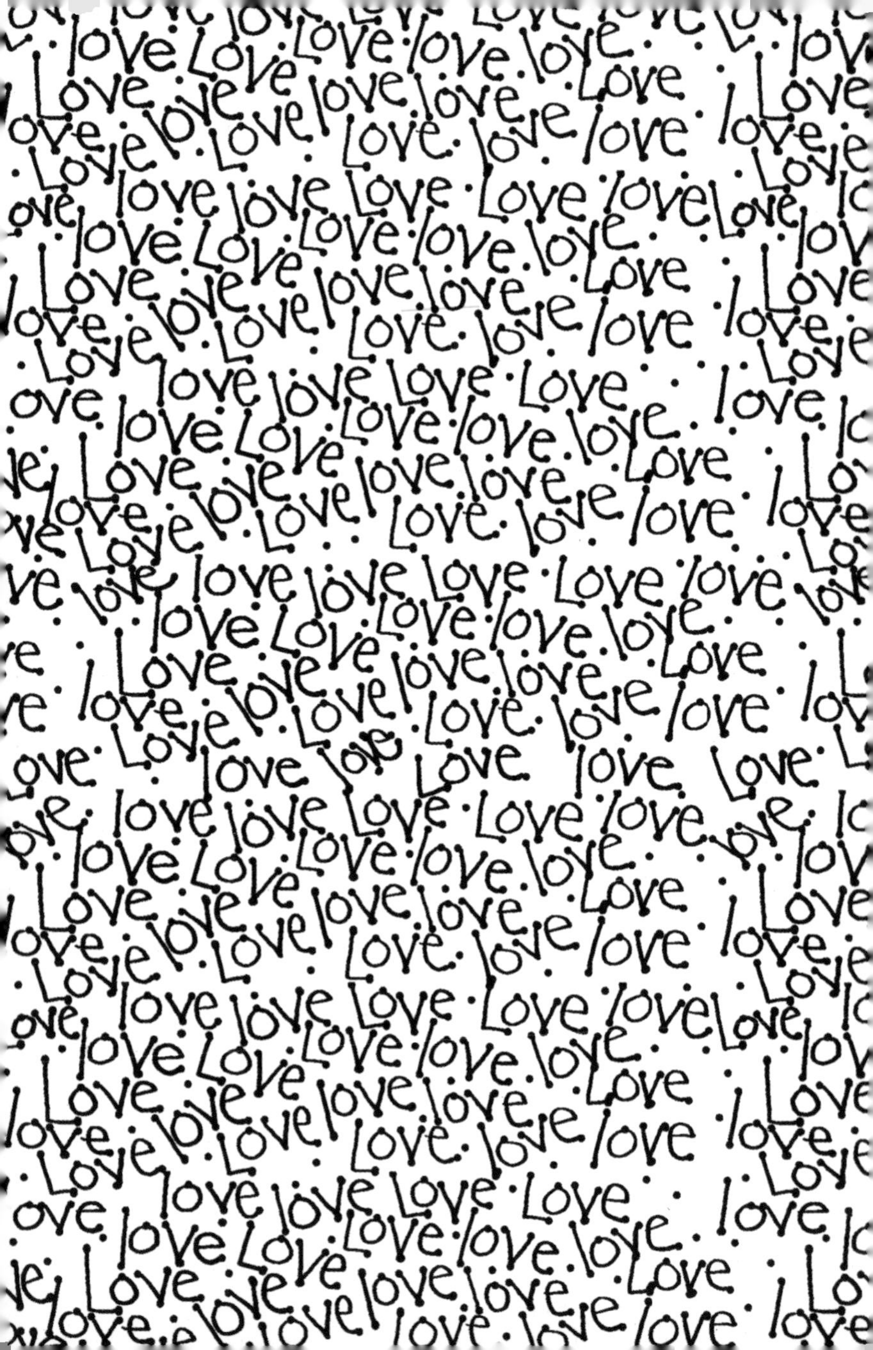

Wherever I go...
Whatever I do...
I carry your love in my heart.
It is a treasure I cherish
and appreciate more every day.

Blue Mountain Arts, Inc.

P.O. Box 4549, Boulder, Colorado 80306

I Love You More Every Day

Our Love Is a Treasure

Marci

Blue Mountain Press™
Boulder, Colorado

I Love You
More
Every
Day

I love you more every day, and as time passes I realize just how blessed I am to have you as my partner. The journey of life, with its ups and downs, has made me appreciate the treasure in our love. The passing of time has given us a book of memories to hold dear. Thank you for bringing love into my life.

When I am with you, I am home... for home is the place where the best memories are made... where I can be "me" and know I am loved. Your love has allowed me to see the best parts of myself because there is a constancy I have come to rely on. I am grateful to you for our special times together and for making all my dreams come true. You are my perfect match.

I Cannot
Remember
a Time You
Were Not
a Part
of My
Life

I can't remember when exactly I fell in love with you. I cannot remember a time you were not a part of my life. You are my companion, my helpmate, my friend. Even though there are struggles — ups and downs, joys and sorrows — I know you are always there. The commitment that you live brings my greatest joy and allows me to experience unconditional love.

When I consider all the people in all the world I could have fallen in love with, I feel like the luckiest person on earth. We have so much in common... We enjoy life in the same way... We have the same values and goals. If there is such a thing as destiny, I know you are mine!

Love

If I searched the world, I could never find a better partner. You are a perfect example of loving and caring and compassion and concern. Just talking to you can make me feel better, and being with you reminds me of the most important things in life.

Love

Love

You Are the Person of My Dreams

Every dream I have ever had about the person I want to spend my life with includes you. All my needs, all my wants, and all my desires are wrapped up in you. I could never ask for a more perfect love, a feeling of being so complete, or a satisfaction so total.

It's All
Because
of
You...

Because of you, I know what it means to love completely... You have taken me to a place I thought existed only in dreams.

Because of you, I have someone to share the simple things... Your commitment to our life makes everything special.

Because of you, I have someone to share my dreams... The stars are within reach with you by my side.

Because of you, I wake each day knowing I am truly loved... There is no better gift in this world than that.

Our Love
Gets Better
All the Time

When I first fell in love with you, I thought nothing could be better. But I have found that time has given us a richer and deeper love... a love that comes with a sense of pride and satisfaction. It's not just the good things we've shared that make our love what it is, but the rewards we get from navigating the obstacles in our journey and arriving at a stronger relationship. My life is so much more than I could have ever imagined because you are in it... You are the other half of my heart, my partner in life.

When I am with you it feels like everything is right with the world... and even when we're not together, thoughts of you are never far. The special moments we've shared, the laughs that keep us grounded, and the love that seals our everlasting bond come together to create a feeling of happiness that sustains me through all that life brings. I thank the stars for letting you fall from the sky like a bright light into my life.

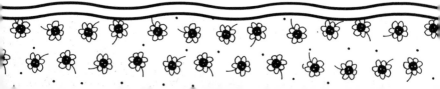

You are the one who believes in me no matter what... who celebrates my strengths and doesn't seem to notice my weaknesses... who is there for me through thick and thin, always inspiring me to do my best. I can count on you to be the one who says, "You can do it"... "Hang in there"... and "Everything's going to be okay." I hope you know how very much this means to me.

You're My
One
and
Only

When we are very young, we begin to think about finding someone to spend our lives with. We imagine falling in love, and we believe that when we do, our lives will be complete. You are the one who fulfills that dream for me... and "falling" in love with you is the most exciting thing that has ever happened to me. "Being" in love with you each and every day is what completes me. You are my dream. You are my one and only.

I Feel Blessed
Every Day
to Have
You in
My Life

Only my heart can truly express just how much you mean to me. You are the light that shines in my life when I need inspiration... Yours are the arms that hug me when I need consoling... You are the person I rely on to listen when I just need to be heard... You are the one who says the things I most need to hear. I feel blessed each and every day to have you in my life.

Let's Make a Promise To...

1. Hold hands, no matter how old we are.

2. Say "I love you" every day.

3. Write love notes for each other to find.

4. Forget mistakes.

5. Forgive words spoken too soon.

6. Plan time alone together.

7. Focus on the things we like about each other.

8. Not expect perfection.

9. Try to be the person of each other's dreams.

10. Support each other through life's challenges.

11. Say "thank you" often.

12. Send text messages that say "I love you."

13. Take walks together.

14. Hug and kiss every day.

I Want to Share Every Part of My Life With You

I want to share my life
with you...
every joy,
every sorrow,
every triumph,
every challenge,
every hope,
every dream,
every good thing
and every hard thing,
knowing our love will
endure that test of time
and give us each
the strength to overcome
any obstacle that comes our way.

There's Nothing We Can't Do Together

We may not have always understood the gift wrapped up in a greater plan. Time has taught us about the bond of love. We have learned together, sharing the good times and the bad, and no matter what, there has always been love.

With Each
Passing Day
My Love
for You
Grows

As time passes I realize how blessed I am to have you as my partner. I can see how much you love me when you look at me, and I can feel that love with your embrace. The journey of life and the passing of time have made me appreciate the treasure in our love and all that you are to me.

Wherever I go... whatever I do...
I carry your love in my heart.
Your love becomes hope and
makes life's challenges bearable.
Your love becomes faith and
inspires me to do my best. Your
love stays in my heart each
and every hour of the day and
reminds me that I am not alone.

Your love is the most important thing in my life. When I am with you, the past and the future lose all meaning, as the "present" with you is truly a gift.

Love is the
greatest gift
of all.

Let's Always Remember How Important Our Relationship Is

Let's always remember to thank each other for the gift of our love. Some believe love means "happily ever after," but we know that is the end result of living "one day at a time." We will experience love and joy, sorrow and pain. Let's promise to enjoy the good times and step through the tough times, remembering that our lives have been brought together for a reason, and that is our spiritual growth. Let's rejoice in the endless possibilities to extend ourselves in love and commit to the task. Let's learn to experience unconditional love and give thanks for our everlasting bond.

You Will
Always
Be
the
One
I Love

You are everything I could ever want, and when I look back, it seems as though my life began the day I met you. You are there when I need support... you believe in me when I need inspiration... and you love me through all times. You are the most important part of my life.

Our Love
Is a Treasure

Once in a lifetime someone comes into our life that we really connect with heart to heart... soul to soul. A friendship develops and love follows.

With all my being I know that you are my "once in a lifetime," and each time I think of you, I realize how lucky I am to have found you. Thank you for all your love... thank you for all that you are... thank you for being a part of my life each and every day! I love you!

About Marci

Marci began her career by hand painting floral designs on clothing. No one was more surprised than she was when one day, in a single burst of inspiration and a completely new and different art style, her delightful characters sprang from her pen! "Their wild and crazy hair is a sign of strength," she thought, "and their crooked little smiles are endearing." She quickly identified the charming characters as Mother, Daughter, Sister, Father, Son, Friend, and so on until all the people and places in life were filled. Then, with her own loved ones in mind, she wrote a true and special sentiment to each one. This would be the beginning of a wonderful success story, which today still finds Marci writing each and every one of her verses in this same personal way.

Marci is a self-taught artist who has always enjoyed writing and art. She is thrilled to see how her delightful characters and universal messages of love have touched the hearts and lives of people everywhere. Her distinctive designs can also be found on Blue Mountain Arts greeting cards, calendars, bookmarks, and other gift items.

To learn more about Marci, look for Children of the Inner Light on Facebook or visit her website: www.MARCIonline.com.